ISBN 978-1-331-80139-9
PIBN 10236521

This book is a reproduction of an important historical work. Forgotten Books uses state-of-the-art technology to digitally reconstruct the work, preserving the original format whilst repairing imperfections present in the aged copy. In rare cases, an imperfection in the original, such as a blemish or missing page, may be replicated in our edition. We do, however, repair the vast majority of imperfections successfully; any imperfections that remain are intentionally left to preserve the state of such historical works.

English
Français
Deutsche
Italiano
Español
Português

www.forgottenbooks.com

Mythology Photography **Fiction**
Fishing Christianity **Art** Cooking
Essays Buddhism Freemasonry
Medicine **Biology** Music **Ancient
Egypt** Evolution Carpentry Physics
Dance Geology **Mathematics** Fitness
Shakespeare **Folklore** Yoga Marketing
Confidence Immortality Biographies
Poetry **Psychology** Witchcraft
Electronics Chemistry History **Law**
Accounting **Philosophy** Anthropology
Alchemy Drama Quantum Mechanics
Atheism Sexual Health **Ancient History**
Entrepreneurship Languages Sport
Paleontology Needlework Islam
Metaphysics Investment Archaeology
Parenting Statistics Criminology
Motivational

References showing the Scriptural Basis of some of the ·Christian Doctrines of the Religious Society of Friends ∴ ∴ ∴ ∴

PHILADELPHIA, PA.

1902

The following selections of Scripture texts and references to writings bearing upon, and explanatory of, some views of Christian Doctrine held by the Religious Society of Friends, have been prepared in response to inquiries and in the hope of aiding the Officers and Teachers of our First Day Schools clearly to present these views, as the subjects treated of may claim the attention of their scholars, or other fitting occasions offer.

They are commended to them, and to thoughtful inquirers everywhere, by the Executive Committee of Friends' First Day School Association of Philadelphia and its vicinity.

Deut. iv: 9.

The Holy Spirit.

BASIC TEXTS : — Job xxxii : 8 ; Joel ii : 28, 29 ; John i : 9, xvi : 13-15.

Especial stress is laid by Friends upon the office of the Holy Spirit in His relation to every human soul.

This relation has been variously expressed as "the Inner Light," "the Light within," "the Indwelling Christ."

OTHER TEXTS : — 1 Kings xix : 12 ; Psalms cxxxix : 7; Isaiah lvii : 15; lxi : 1; Ezek. xxxvi: 26, 27; Matt. x : 20; Luke xi : 35; John iii : 8, iv : 24; vi : 63, xiv : 16-20 ; xv : 26; 1 Cor. xv : 45; II Cor. iii: 6; Eph. i: 17, ii: 1, 18, iv. 30-32, v: 18; 1 John i: 5, iv: 2, v 6-8; James i: 21 ; Rev. xxii: 17.

The subject treated of in the following :--

"Barclay's Apology;" Prop. vi, particularly Sec. 11,

"Quaker Strongholds;" Chap. ii. (Caroline E. Stephen),

"The distinguishing doctrines of the Society of Friends" (James Wood),

"Encyclopædia Britannica," Art. "The Quakers,"

"Sewell's History," Chap. i, page 38 (Ed. 1871).

Divine Worsbip.

BASIC TEXTS :—* John iv : 24; † Matt. xviii: 20.

OTHER TEXTS:—Psalms lxii: 5, lxvi: 1, 2, 4, 8, 9, 13ff; Isaiah xli: 1; Zech. ii: 10, 13; Hab. ii: 20; Acts iv: 31, xii: 5, 12, xx : 7; I Cor. xii : 27-31, xiv : 26, 29-33.

The subject treated of in the following:—
" Barclay's Apology; " Chapter on Worship,
" Reasons for the Necessity of Silent Waiting in order to the Solemn Worship of God " (Mary Brook),

" The Distinguishing Doctrines of the Religious Society of Friends " pages 11-15 (James Wood),

" Dynamic Faith; " pages 30, 37ff., 77ff. (Rufus M. Jones),

" Quaker Strongholds; " pages 51-83 (Caroline E. Stephen),

" Four Lectures on Some of the Distinguishing Views of Friends " pages 75-88 (James E. Rhoads).

---

*A proper reading is, " God is Spirit ; " *i e* , of spiritual not material essence.
†" In my name," *i. e.*, in a realization of one's relation to the Father by virtue of the Son.

Vocal Ministry and the Priesthood of Believers.

MINISTRY.

BASIC TEXTS:—Matt. iv: 19, x : 7, 8.

" It is the prerogative of Jesus Christ our Lord to choose and put forth his own ministers. A clear apprehension of Scripture doctrine or a heart enlarged in love to others is not of itself sufficient for this work.

" All true ministry of the Gospel is from the appointment of the Lord Jesus Christ, and it is He, who by His Spirit prepares and qualifies for the work. The gift must be exercised in continued dependence upon Him,—and blessed is that ministry in which man is humbled and Christ and His grace exalted.

" Gifts, precious as they may be, must not be mistaken for grace. They add to our responsibility but they do not raise the minister above his brethren."—(*London Yearly Meeting Printed Epistles, 1835, 42, 71, 76.*)

OTHER TEXTS:—Exodus iv: 12; Isaiah : 4; Jer. i: 7, 9 ; John xiv: 16, 17; Matt. x: 19, 20 ; Luke, xxi: 15; Acts ii: 4, 16-18, viii: 20; I Cor. ii:4-13; I John ii: 27.

THE PRIESTHOOD OF BELIEVERS.

BASIC TEXTS:—Heb. iii: 1; I Peter ii: 5, 9; Rev. i: 6.

he subject treated of in the following

Barclay's Apology;" Chap. on Min

A Concise Account of the Religious *

riends" (Thomas Evans), Tracts 24 *

Ministry,

Quaker Strongholds" (Caroline E. St

'Friends in the Seventeenth Cent

.arles Evans), Chapters iv, vi.

Women's Ministry in the Gospel
of Our
Lord and Saviour Jesus Christ.

BASIC TEXTS: — Isaiah liv: 13; Joel ii: 28, 29; Gal. iii: 28; I Cor. xii: 13.

OTHER TEXTS:—Rom. x: xii: 4, 5; Eph. iv: 4, 11, 16; Col. iii.^{12}11 ; Acts ii: 16-18; Judges iv: 4, 5, v; II Kings xxii: 14-19; Acts xxi: 8, 9; Luke ii: 36; i: 46-55; Rom. xvi: 1-6; Phil. iv: 3.

The subject treated of in the following :—

" Barclay's Apology; " Prop. x (end of Sec. 27).

" Observations on Friends" Chap. viii. (J. J. Gurney),

"A Portraiture of Quakerism," Chap. x., Vol. ii. (Thomas Clarkson),

" Collateral Testimonies to Quaker Principles," Chap. ii. (Mary E. Beck).

Baptism.

BASIC TEXTS :—Matt. iii : 11; I Peter iii: 21; Titus iii: 5-7.

The Religious Society of Friends holds that the baptism which now saves is inward and spiritual; " one spirit into one body " : that " as many as are baptized into Christ have put on Christ; " and that " if any man be in Christ, he is a new creature; old things are passed away ; behold all things are become new, and all things of God."

OTHER TEXTS:—I Cor. xii : 13; Gal. iii: 27; II Cor. v: 17, 18.

The subject treated of in the following:—
" Barclay's Apology; " (Chapter on Baptism),
" A Concise Account of the Religious Society of Friends," pages 42, 43 (Thomas Evans),
" Baptism and the Supper; " (a small book by J. J. Gurney),
" The True Christian Baptism and Communion " (Joseph Phipps),
" The True Christian Baptism Not of Water;" Tract No. 60 (Enoch Lewis).

The Lord's Supper.

BASIC TEXTS :—Matt. xxvi : 26-28 ; Mark xiv: 22-24; Luke xxii: 19-20; I Cor. xi: 23-26.

OTHER TEXTS :—John vi: 48, 53-58 ; I Cor. x : 16, 21.

The subject treated of in the following :—
" George Fox's Journal," pp. 247f., 300f.
" George Fox's Epistles,"
" Barclay's Apology; " Prop. xiii,
" The Distinguishing Doctrines of the Religious Society of Friends," pp. 24ff. (James Wood),
" The True Christian Baptism and Communion," p. 35ff. (Joseph Phipps),
" Quaker Strongholds; " p. 88ff. (Caroline E. Stephen),
" The True Christian Communion," Tract No. 154,
" Baptism and the Supper " (a small book by J. J. Gurney).

BASIC TEXTS :—James iv : 1 ; Matt.
v: 43ff.

———

OTHER TEXTS :—Isaiah ii: 4, lx: 18;
John xv: 12; Eph. iv: 2, 3; Rom. xii: 20;
II Tim. ii: 22; II Cor. x: 4; Matt. v: 21,
22, xxvi: 52.

The subject treated of in the following :—

"Argument on Causes, Consequences and
Lawfulness of War" (Jonathan Dymond),

"The Rights of Self-Defence" (Jonathan
Dymond),

"Military Glory" (Jonathan Dymond),

"The Primitive Christians' Estimate of War
and Self-Defence" (Josiah W. Leeds),

Papers issued by Philadelphia Yearly Meeting,

"An Address on the Subject of War" (1887)

"An Appeal to Christians in Regard to War"
(1896),

"A Plea in Behalf of Peace" (1900).

Oaths.

All Christian denominations hold that profanity is wrong. The view of Friends which distinguishes them from others is, that they hold that all oaths whatsoever are forbidden under the Christian dispensation. They believe that the words of Christ, as given in the basic texts, are clear and unmistakable. He said "swear not at all." James in his Epistle uses nearly the same language. Friends do not believe that legal or confirmatory oaths are excepted from these scriptural injunctions.

In the early years of the society Friends suffered greatly because of this testimony. Many were kept in filthy prisons for years, and some ended their lives in these dungeons rather than transgress what they believed was the command of Christ."

There is no doubt that the teachings of Friends on this subject have wrought a great change in public opinion, and now in the United States and in the British Dominions, any one who has conscientious scruples against taking an oath, is at liberty to affirm.

The subject treated of in the following :—

" Barclay's Apology," Prop. xv, Sec. 10,

Publications referred to in the foregoing notes can be purchased as follows.—

At FRIENDS' BOOK STORE, No. 304 Arch Street, Philadelphia.

" Barclay's Apology."

" A Concise Account of the Religious Society of Friends."

" The True Christian Baptism and Communion."

" George Fox's Journal " and " Epistles."

" Reasons for the Necessity of Silent Waiting in order to the Solemn Worship of God."

" Friends in the Seventeenth Century."

" Penn's Rise and Progress."

Tracts Nos. 24, 60, 82 and 154.

Addresses of Philadelphia Yearly Meeting.

Jonathan Dymond's works.

At FRIENDS' BOOK AND TRACT COMMIT-TEE, No. 51, Fifth Avenue, New York.

" Dynamic Faith."

." The Distinguishing Doctrines of the Religious Society of Friends."

At FRIENDS' INSTITUTE, No. 20 South Twelfth Street, Philadelphia.

"Collateral Testimonies to Quaker Principles. '

" Observations on Friends."

" Baptism and the Supper."

" Four Lectures on Some of the Distinguish-ing Views of Friends."

" Quaker Strongholds."

" Quaker Strongholds " (War, pp. 129-140).

Proposition xv., Sec. 6, " Barclay's Apology " (Revenge and War).

Proceedings of the late Peace Conference Philadelphia.

CPSIA information can be obtained
at www.ICGtesting.com
Printed in the USA
BVHW040819220219
540922BV00024B/2822/P